Inventors and Inventions

Guided/Group Reading Notes

White Band

Contents

Introduction 2

Guided/Group reading notes

① Character story: *Underwater Adventure*
by Tony Bradman 12

② Character story: *Cuckoo Trouble*
by Tony Bradman 18

③ Character story: *Ant and the Break-bot*
by Chris Powling 24

④ Character non-fiction: *Flying Machines*
by John Malam 30

⑤ Variety non-fiction: *Extreme Exploring Machines*
by Alison Blank 36

OXFORD

Introduction

Reading progression at age 6–7

At age 6–7, children begin to read independently using longer texts containing both familiar words and unfamiliar words that are not completely decodable. The texts at **white band** are slightly longer than those at gold band but still contain a core of high and medium frequency words and phonetically regular words to support the children as they build reading confidence and fluency. New vocabulary is introduced within the context of familiar words.

> The range of genres and writing styles continues to expand. A story line or theme may be sustained over a longer period of time and simple 'non-chronological' plots will be introduced with clear pointers for the reader about changes in, or passage of, time.

The characters continue to develop in complexity and more than one point of view is expressed within the text. Information or action is increasingly implied rather than spelled out. Sentence structure will be longer and more subordinate phrases or clauses are included. Similes and metaphors, as well as technical language where appropriate, are used. Examples of 'literary' language are frequent.

A range of non-fiction features including charts, maps, labelled diagrams, captions, index and glossaries are used to encourage the children to read and interpret information presented in a variety of ways.

A closer look at Opportunity

Panoramic camera

Solar panels: provide power

Six sturdy wheels: to travel over the rocky surface

Robot arm: for lifting tools

Visual literacy is supported through additional action and information in the illustrations and photographs, and the suggestions for visualization comprehension strategies suggested in these notes.

Progression in the Project X character books

In this cluster, there is a two-part story in which the children continue to use the shrinking power of the watches. In *Underwater Adventure*, Tiger loses his watch at the bottom of the pond and Max and Ant use their latest invention – the Super-Micro Submarine – to try to retrieve it. All does not go to plan, but in the second book, *Cuckoo Trouble*, Tiger and Cat use their ingenuity to rescue the boys. In the third character story, *Ant and the Break-bot*, their micro-size helps the children to participate in a robot competition. Their lack of practice leads to disaster but their excellent design is recognized and rewarded.

Guided/Group reading

The engaging content and careful levelling of Project X books makes them ideal for use in guided/group reading sessions. The advantages of using guided/group reading, as well as charts to help you assess the appropriate level for a reading group, are discussed in the *Teaching Handbook Age 6–7* (Year 2/P3).

To use the books in guided/group reading sessions, you should select a book at a band that creates a small degree of challenge for the group of pupils. Typically, the children should be able to read about 90% of the book unaided. This level of 'readability' provides the context for the children to practise their reading and build reading confidence. The 'challenge' in the text provides opportunities for explicitly teaching reading skills.

These *Guided/Group Reading Notes* provide support for each book in the cluster, along with suggestions for follow-up activities. Books at white band can be covered in one or two reading guided/group reading sessions. Alternatively, the children may read much of each book independently.

Speaking, listening and drama

Talk is crucial to learning. Children need plenty of opportunities to express their ideas through talk and drama, and to listen to and watch the ideas of others. These processes are important for building reading engagement, personal response and understanding. Suggestions for speaking, listening and drama are given for every book.

> Within these *Guided/Group Reading Notes* the speaking and listening activities are linked to the reading assessment focuses.

Building comprehension

Understanding what we have read is at the heart of reading. To help readers become effective in comprehending a text these *Guided/Group Reading Notes* contain practical strategies to develop the following important aspects of comprehension:

- Previewing
- Predicting
- Activating and building prior knowledge
- Questioning
- Recalling
- Visualizing and other sensory responses
- Deducing, inferring and drawing conclusions
- Determining importance
- Synthesizing
- Empathizing
- Summarizing
- Personal response, including adopting a critical stance.

The research basis and rationale for focusing on these aspects of comprehension is given in the *Teaching Handbook Age 6–7* (Year 2/P3).

Reading fluency

Reading fluency combines automatic word recognition, reading with pace and expression. Rereading, fluency and building comprehension are linked together in a complex interrelationship, where each supports the other. This is discussed more fully in the *Teaching Handbook Age 6–7* (Year 2/P3). Opportunities for the children to read aloud are important in building fluency and reading aloud to the children provides models of expressive fluent reading. Suggestions for purposeful and enjoyable oral reading and rereading/re-listening activities are given in the follow-up activities in these *Guided/Group Reading Notes* and in the notes for parents on the inside cover of each book.

The Project X *Interactive Stories* software can be used to provide a model of reading fluency for the whole class and/or opportunities for individuals or small groups of the children to listen to texts. Listening to stories being read is particularly effective with EAL children.

Building vocabulary

Explicit work on enriching vocabulary is important in building reading fluency and comprehension. Repeatedly encountering a word and its variants helps it become known on sight. The thematic 'cluster' structure of Project X supports this because words are repeated within and across the books. Suggestions for vocabulary work are included in these notes. The vocabulary chart on pages 10 and 11 shows when vocabulary is repeated and new words are introduced. It also indicates those words that can be used to support learning alongside a structured phonics and spelling programme.

Developing a thematic approach

Helping the children make links in their learning supports their development as learners. All the books in this cluster focus on the theme **Inventors and Inventions**. A chart showing the cross-curricular potential of this theme is given in the *Teacher's Resource Book Age 6–9 – More Purple to Grey Clusters*. Some suggestions for cross-curricular activities are also given in these *Guided/Group Reading Notes*, in the follow-up suggestions for each book.

In guided/group reading sessions, you will also want to encourage children to make links between the books in the cluster. Grouping books in a cluster allows readers to make links between characters, events and actions across the books. This enables readers gradually to build complex understandings of characters, to give reasons why things happen and how characters may change and develop. It can help them recognize cause and effect. It helps the children reflect on the skill of determining importance, as a minor incident or detail in one book may prove to have greater significance when considered across several books.

Note that the books in this cluster can mostly be read in any order. In the two-part character story, *Underwater Adventure* should be read before *Cuckoo Trouble*.

In the **Inventors and Inventions** cluster, some of the suggested links that can be explored across the books include:

- designing a machine for exploring an extreme environment **(DT)**
- looking at forces related to cogs and wheels **(Science)**
- exploring manufactured robots that use control technology **(ICT)**
- finding out about the history of flying. **(History)**

Reading into writing

The Project X books provide both models and inspiration to support the children's writing. Brief suggestions for relevant, contextualized and interesting writing activities are given in the follow-up activities for each book. These include both short and longer writing opportunities. The activities cover a wide range of writing contexts so writers can develop an understanding of adapting their writing for different audiences and purposes.

The Project X *Interactive Stories* software contains a collection of 'clip art' assets from the character books – characters, settings and props – that the children can use in their writing. There are also a number of writing frames and activity sheets for pupils to follow or use, or that pupils can write/type into directly to practise writing and ICT skills.

Selecting follow-up activities

These *Guided/Group Reading Notes* give many ideas for follow-up activities. Some of these can be completed within the guided/group reading session. Some are longer activities that will need to be worked on over time. You should select those activities that are most appropriate for your pupils. It is not expected that you would complete all the suggested activities.

Home/school reading

Books used in a guided/group reading session can also be used in home/school reading programmes.

Before a guided/group reading session, the child could:

- read the first chapter or section of a book
- read a related book from the cluster to build background knowledge.

Following a guided/group reading session, the child could:

- reread the book at home to build reading confidence and fluency
- read the next chapter or section in a longer book
- read a related book from the cluster.

Advice for parents on supporting their child in reading at home is provided on the inside covers of individual books. There is further advice for teachers concerning home/school reading partnerships in the *Teaching Handbook Age 6–7* (Year 2/P3).

Assessment

During guided/group reading, teachers make ongoing assessments of individuals and of the group. Reading targets are indicated for each book and you should assess against these reading targets. You should select just one or two targets at a time as the focus for the group. The same target can be appropriate for several literacy sessions or over several texts.

Readers should be encouraged to self-assess and peer-assess against the target/s.

Further support for assessing pupils' progress is provided in the *Teaching Handbook Age 6–7* (Year 2/P3).

Continuous reading objectives and ongoing assessment

The following objectives will be supported in *every* guided/group reading session and are therefore a *continuous* focus for attention and assessment (AF1). These objectives are not listed in full for each book but as you listen to individual the children reading you should undertake ongoing assessment against these decoding and encoding objectives:

- Read independently and with increasing fluency longer and less familiar texts **5.1**
- Know how to tackle unfamiliar words that are not completely decodable **5.3**
- Read and spell less common alternative graphemes including trigraphs **5.4**
- Read high and medium frequency words independently and automatically **5.5**

Further objectives are provided as a focus within the notes for each book, as appropriate, from these strands:

- Understanding and interpreting texts (*Strand 7*)
- Engaging with and responding to texts (*Strand 8*)

Correlation to the specific objectives/guidelines within Scottish, Welsh and Northern Irish curricula are provided in the *Teacher's Resource Book Age 6–9 – More Purple to Grey Clusters*.

Recording assessment

The assessment chart for the **Inventors and Inventions** cluster is provided in the *Teacher's Resource Book Age 6–9 – More Purple to Grey Clusters*.

Diagnostic assessment

If an individual child is failing to make good progress or he or she seems to have a specific problem with some aspect of reading you will want to undertake a more detailed assessment. Details of how to use running records for diagnostic assessment and resource sheets for undertaking such assessments are given in the *Teaching Handbook Age 6–7* (Year 2/P3).

Vocabulary chart

At age 6–7, the children should:

- read high and medium frequency words independently and automatically
- read and spell
    - less common alternative graphemes
    - compound words and polysyllabic words
    - suffixes and prefixes.

NB There are too many common high frequency words in each book to list them all. The first 100 words are known by this stage. A selection is given from the final 200 words in the *300 common words in order of frequency* list. Examples only are given of the categories of words listed above.

Underwater Adventure	High frequency words	going, can't, cried, because, would, we're, looking, park
	Phonetically regular compound and polysyllabic words	hanging, metal, airlock, clockwork
	Alternative graphemes for the same phoneme, including trigraphs	/er/ (er, ur, or, ir): perfect, certain, surface, urgently, clockwork, first /oo/ (oo, u, o-e, ough): room, cuckoo, zoom, super, lose, through
	Context vocabulary	submarine, periscope, water-beetle, cuckoo, murky, tangled
Cuckoo Trouble	High frequency words	friends, can't, inside, food, through, thought, going, know, pulled
	Phonetically regular compound and polysyllabic words	ticking, darkness, window
	Alternative graphemes for the same phoneme, including trigraphs	/ai/ (a, ai, ay, a-e, ea, aigh, eigh): amazing, explain, playing, escape, break, straight, weight /ee/ (e, ee, ea, ie): he, weeds, reveal, grease, piece /or/ (or, aw, au, ough): for, claw, launched, thought
	Context vocabulary	cuckoo clock, airlock, engine, pedal, cog, handles

Ant and the Break-bot	High frequency words	never, first, couldn't, garden, everyone, around
	Phonetically regular compound and polysyllabic words	competition, tickets, robot, Spangler, plastic, finished
	Alternative graphemes for the same phoneme	/s/ (s, ss, c, ce): special, pressed, cinema, dance /ee/ (ee, e, ea, e-e, ie, ey, y): free, maybe, reading, completely, Katie, curtsey, Lucy, Beauty-bot
	Context vocabulary	break-dancing, tubing, judges
Flying Machines	High frequency words	why, when, would, after, before, began, birds, fly
	Phonetically regular compound and polysyllabic words	inventor, helicopter, hundred, propeller, enemy, factory, notebooks, airstrip, airshows
	Alternative graphemes for the same phoneme, including trigraphs	/igh/ (i, igh, y, ie, i-e, eigh): idea, flight, fly, died, spitfire, height /or/ (or, ore, our) story, before, four
	Context vocabulary	inventor, helicopter, rotor, glider, biplane, engine, propellers, mission, souvenirs, airshows, ammunition, UAV
Extreme Exploring Machines	High frequency words	many, water, inside, find, which, once, where
	Phonetically regular compound and polysyllabic words	robot, toxic, explorer, volcanic, amazing, equipment, Titanic, underwater, onboard
	Alternative graphemes for the same phoneme	/ai/ (a, ai, ay, a-e): volcano, contain, layers, x-ray, days, earthquake, safely, lake /dj/ (g, ge, j): engineer, geothermal, wreckage, July, journey
	Context vocabulary	submersible, wreckage, geothermal, acrylic, data, solar panels, hydrogen, trigger, tsunamis, earthquakes, micro-organisms

Underwater Adventure

BY TONY BRADMAN

About this book

Tiger loses his watch in the pond in the park. Luckily, Max and Ant have been working on a new invention – a Super Micro-Submarine. They dive to the bottom of the pond to rescue the watch but all does not go to plan.

Writing genres: narrative

You will need

- *Prediction and reflection grid* Photocopy Master 82, *Teaching Handbook Age 6–7* (Year 2/P3)
- *First and third person words* Photocopy Master 16, *Teacher's Resource Book Age 6–9*
- *My invention* Photocopy Master 17, *Teacher's Resource Book Age 6–9*

	Literacy Framework objective	Target and assessment focus
Speaking, listening, group interaction and drama	○ Adopt appropriate roles in small or large groups and consider alternative courses of action **4.1**	○ We can use drama strategies to help us to predict what might happen in the story **AF3**
Reading	○ Engage with books through exploring and enacting interpretations **8.2**	○ We can use information from the book to explain why people say the things they do **AF2**
	○ Explore how particular words are used **7.5**	○ We can identify words written in the third person **AF5**
Writing	○ Sustain form in narative, including use of person and time **9.2**	○ We can write a scene in the third person using words such as 'he' and 'she' **AF7**

Before reading

To activate prior knowledge and encourage prediction

- Ask the children to notice who is on the front cover. Where are Max and Ant? (underwater) **(activating prior knowledge)**
- What sort of adventures might they have underwater? **(predicting)**

To preview the text

- Read up to page 6 to the children. Talk to them about the story so far. Point out that it seems to have nothing to do with being underwater. **(previewing)**
- How do they think this section might lead into an underwater adventure? **(predicting)**

To support decoding and word recognition and introduce new vocabulary

- **Phonic opportunity** Revisit *-ed* endings with the children. Can they spot any in the story? e.g. *asked* (p.6), *arrived* (p.8), *moaned* (p.9), *disappeared* (p.10). Ask them to collect the words and make a display, drawing them inside a large outline of a submarine.
- You may also wish to point out some of the high or medium frequency words or practise decoding some of the phonically regular words in this book and listed in the vocabulary chart on page 10.
- Before children read independently, ask them to rehearse what they might do if they become stuck on a word or sentence. The range of possible strategies (such as rereading, reading on, using context, using phonic, syntactic and vocabulary knowledge) should be well established for most readers and only an occasional reminder should be necessary.

During reading

- Ask the children to read from page 7 to the end of the book.
- As they read, ask them to find words which are used in the story to show it is written in the third person, e.g. 'he' and 'she' rather than 'I'.
- Stress the importance of comprehension, reminding the children to stop and take action if they are failing to understand the text, e.g. checking the meaning of a particular word or phrase, rereading more carefully, reading on to see if the meaning becomes clear, reading it aloud, discussing the passage with someone, etc.

> **Assessment point**
>
> Listen to individual children reading and make ongoing assessments on their decoding, sight vocabulary, approaches to tackling new words and their reading fluency. AF1

 After reading

Returning to the text
- How did Tiger lose his watch? **(recall)**
- Why does Ant say to Tiger *"We wouldn't want you to break anything"*? **(deducing, inferring and drawing conclusions)**
- How do they think Tiger feels when the other children say he might break things? **(empathizing)**

> **Assessment point**
>
> Can the children identify reasons why the characters say the things they do to each other? AF2

- Why do they think the cuckoo clock might be important to the story? **(synthesizing, deducing, inferring and drawing conclusions)**

Building comprehension

- Ask the children, in small groups, to create a freeze frame image of the last scene in the book, where Max and Ant are trapped in the submarine whilst Cat and Tiger are at the edge of the pond. Tap the children on the shoulder and ask them to describe what they are thinking. Once they have shared their thoughts in role, let them explore the next story through role play. What do they think will happen next? How will Tiger help them out of their sticky situation? **(personal response, determining importance, predicting)**

> **Assessment point**
>
> Can the children use drama to predict what might happen next, justifying their reasons? AF3

- Ask the children to fill in the *Prediction and reflection grid* Photocopy Master to consider what might happen in the next book (*Cuckoo Trouble*). They can fill in the last section when they read *Cuckoo Trouble*. **(deducing, inferring, predicting)**

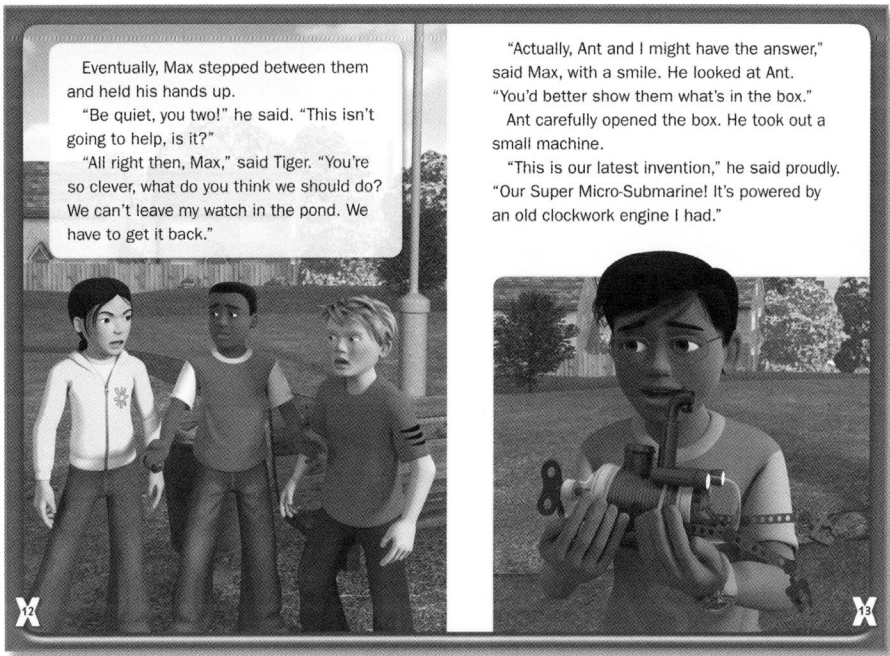

Building vocabulary

- Ask the children to carry out a detective hunt to collect words that show which person (first and third) the story is written in.

- Give the children the *First and third person words* Photocopy Master to help them sort first and third person words.

..................................>

> **Assessment point**
> Can the children identify the words written in the first and third person? **AF5**

- Ask the children to use a computer to write a scene from *Underwater Adventure* in the third person in their own words. Then ask them to highlight all the third person words in green on the screen.

..................................>

> **Assessment point**
> Can the children use the correct pronouns, verb forms, etc. when writing a scene in the third person? **AF7**

Follow-up activities

Writing activities

- Ask the children to choose a page of text in the story and help them to turn it into the first person. Which kinds of words did they have to change? **(short writing task)**
- Using their ideas from their earlier role play, ask the children to write a story showing how Tiger might save Max and Ant. Remind the children to write the story in the third person. **(longer writing task)**

- Ask the children to use the *My invention* Photocopy Master to draw and describe an invention of their own that they could use to help someone. **(short writing task)**

Other literacy activities

- Ask the children, in small groups, to retell consecutive chapters to each other in their own words. **(speaking and listening)**

Cross-curricular and thematic opportunities

- Design an underwater vehicle. **(DT)**
- Explore pond habitats to see what other pond life the children in the story might have seen. **(Science)**
- Explore how people's comments make others feel and link this to how Tiger feels when everyone keeps saying he breaks things. **(PSHE)**

Cuckoo Trouble

BY TONY BRADMAN

About this book

This story follows on from *Underwater Adventure* and shows Tiger using his ingenuity to help rescue Max and Ant from the bottom of the pond.

Writing genres: narrative

You will need

- *Long vowel hunt* Photocopy Master 18, *Teacher's Resource Book Age 6–9*
- *What can you see, hear, smell?* Photocopy Master 81, *Teaching Handbook Age 6–7* (Year 2/P3)
- *Story board* Photocopy Master 89, *Teaching Handbook Age 6–7* (Year 2/P3)

	Literacy Framework objective	Target and assessment focus
Speaking, listening, group interaction and drama	○ Speak with clarity and use appropriate intonation when reading and reciting texts **1.1**	○ We can use our voices to build up the tension in the story when reading aloud **AF1**
Reading	○ Explore how particular words are used, including words and expressions with similar meanings **7.5**	○ We can identify descriptive words and phrases that help the reader to imagine the setting **AF5**
	○ Explain their reactions to texts, commenting on important aspects **8.3**	○ We can talk about how the author's choice of words makes us feel **AF6**
Writing	○ Make adventurous word and language choices appropriate to the style and purpose of the text **9.4**	○ We can use descriptive words in our writing to interest the reader **AF7**

Before reading

To activate prior knowledge and encourage prediction

- Ask the children to recap what happened in the previous story *Underwater Adventure*. **(recall, summarizing)**
- Compare the children's versions of the previous story with the summary on pages 2 and 3. Are there any main points they have missed?
- How do they think Tiger is going to save the boys? **(predicting)**

To support decoding and word recognition and introduce new vocabulary

- **Phonic opportunity** Revisit the long vowel phonemes 'ai', 'ee' and 'or'. Give out the *Long vowel hunt* Photocopy Master and ask the children to be word detectives and hunt through the book to find words with these long vowels (see some examples provided in the vocabulary chart on page 10).
- You may also wish to point out some of the high or medium frequency words or practise decoding some of the phonically regular words in this book listed in the vocabulary chart on page 10.
- Before children read independently, ask them to rehearse what they might do if they become stuck on a word or sentence. The range of possible strategies (such as rereading, reading on, using context, using phonic, syntactic and vocabulary knowledge) should be well established for most readers and only an occasional reminder should be necessary.

During reading

- Ask the children to read from page 4 to the end of the book.
- As they read, ask them to notice how the author uses language and descriptive phases to interest the reader, e.g. *"We can climb up the bookcase and then swing across to the clock using the wool like a rope!"* (p.12).
- Stress the importance of comprehension, reminding the children to stop and take action if they are failing to understand the text, e.g. checking the meaning of a particular word or phrase, rereading more carefully, reading on to see if the meaning becomes clear, reading it aloud, discussing the passage with someone, etc.

··➤

Assessment point
Listen to individual children reading and make ongoing assessments on their decoding, sight vocabulary, approaches to tackling new words and their reading fluency. AF1

 After reading

Returning to the text

- Why were Cat and Tiger relieved that Moggy was not in the room? **(deducing, inferring and drawing conclusions)**
- Ask the children how Cat and Tiger managed to get up the bookcase. **(recall)**
- What simile did the author use to describe how high something was? (*"It's as high as a mountain"* on page 11.) Why do they think the author used this phrase? How does it help the reader to imagine the setting? **(determining importance)**

··➤

Assessment point
Can the children talk about how the language used helps the reader to imagine the setting? AF5

Building fluency

- Ask the children, in turn, to read aloud a page each of Chapters 4 and 5, reminding them to build up the tension in the story through the use of their voice.

> **Assessment point**
>
> Can the children use appropriate intonation and expression to depict the tension in the story? AF1

Building comprehension and vocabulary

- The author has decided to help the reader to imagine what it is like by describing what the children could see, hear and smell inside the cuckoo clock. How does this help the reader to imagine a scene? **(synthesizing)**

- Talk about the descriptive words and phrases the children discovered in their reading. Which ones did they like? How did the vocabulary help them to picture the story in their mind? Did any words and phrases evoke particular feelings of fear, excitement, etc.?

- Did the children notice any devices the author used, such as the use of onomatopoeic words (*tick-tick-ticking*) and placing words in capitals and italics (*BOINNNNNNGGGG!*)?

> **Assessment point**
>
> Can the children identify words and phrases that the author uses to evoke an emotional response? AF6

- Ask the children to complete the *What can you see, hear, smell?* Photocopy Master to describe what it might be like if you could shrink and find yourself inside another everyday household object, e.g. a vacuum cleaner, refrigerator, food cupboard, etc. Challenge the children to use descriptive words and phrases. **(visualizing and other sensory responses)**

> **Assessment point**
>
> Can the children begin to use descriptive language to interest the reader? AF7

Follow-up activities

Writing activities

- Ask the children to write speech bubbles for the characters in some of the pictures, then compare them with a partner's. **(short writing task)**
- Ask the children to use their description of a setting to begin a longer imaginative story about a person who shrinks in order to rescue someone. They could use the *Story board* Photocopy Master to help them plan the story. **(longer writing task)**
- Look at how the author has used the word '*Meanwhile*' (on page 20) to allow the reader to find out what is happening to the other characters in the story. Read short sections of the story to the children again, then end the section with the word '*Meanwhile …*'. Ask the children to write what might be going on at this point with the other characters in the story. **(short writing task)**

Other literacy activities

- Ask the children to invent another plan to rescue Max and Ant. Invite them to describe their plan to a partner, who will then explain to someone else how the plan works. Encourage the children to focus on giving precise and clear instructions. **(speaking and listening)**

Cross-curricular and thematic opportunities

- Explore pattern and design using cogs and wheels. **(Art and design)**
- Explore forces related to cogs and wheels. **(Science)**
- Explore the history of the cuckoo clock. **(History)**
- Investigate the similarities and differences between various clocks and devices for telling the time, e.g. wall clock, alarm clock, ship's clock, Grandfather clock, sundial, egg timer, wristwatch. **(DT)**

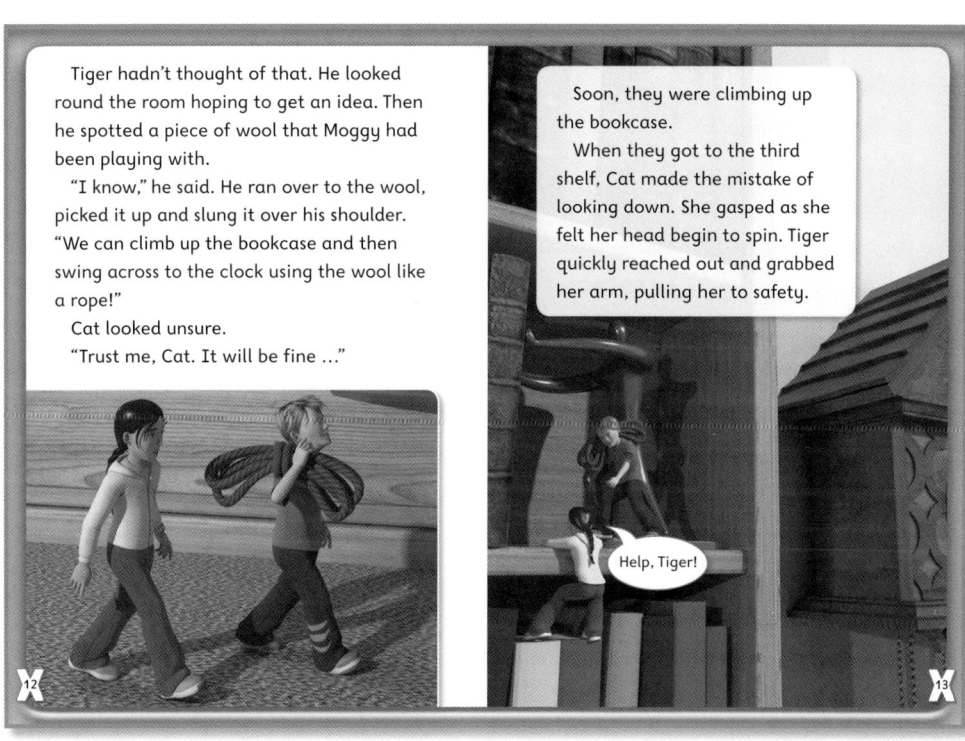

Ant and the Break-bot

BY CHRIS POWLING

About this book
The children have the chance to win free tickets to see the new Robo-Rex film, if they can build an amazing robot. Ant has an idea to build a robot that can break-dance, like himself. Max, Cat and Tiger shrink to help him operate the robot, but disaster strikes on the day of the competition.

Writing genres: narrative, posters, email

You will need
- *Ant's email* Photocopy Master 19, *Teacher's Resource Book Age 6–9*

	Literacy Framework objective	**Target and assessment focus**
Speaking, listening, group interaction and drama	○ Tell real and imagined stories using the conventions of familiar story language **1.2**	○ We can retell the story, using story language **AF2**
Reading	○ Give some reasons why things happen or characters change **7.2** ○ Use syntax and context to build their store of vocabulary when reading for meaning **7.4**	○ We can describe why different things happened in the story **AF2/3** ○ We can read dialogue with expression and confidence to bring out its meaning **AF1**
Writing	○ Select from different presentational features to suit particular writing purposes on paper and on screen **9.5**	○ We can write a response in the form of an email **AF2**

Before reading

To activate prior knowledge

- Talk to the children about entering competitions. Have they ever entered a competition? How did it feel being a competitor? **(activating prior knowledge)**

To preview the text and encourage prediction

- Take a picture walk through the story. What challenges meet the characters? Do they think, based on the pictures, that the story will have a happy ending? **(previewing, predicting)**

To support decoding and word recognition and introduce new vocabulary

- You may wish to point out some of the high or medium frequency words or practise decoding some of the phonically regular words in this book listed in the vocabulary chart on page 11.

To engage readers and support fluent reading

- Look at page 2 and then read the first chapter to the children. Use intonation to build excitement and tension and ask the children to imitate your style of reading by rereading the same section aloud.
- Before children read independently, ask them to rehearse what they might do if they become stuck on a word or sentence. The range of possible strategies (such as rereading, reading on, using context, using phonic, syntactic and vocabulary knowledge) should be well established for most readers and only an occasional reminder should be necessary.

During reading

- Ask the children to read from Chapter 2 to the end of the book.
- As they read, ask them to note what was special about Lucy's robot.
- Stress the importance of comprehension, reminding the children to stop and take action if they are failing to understand the text, e.g. checking the meaning of a particular word or phrase, rereading more carefully, reading on to see if the meaning becomes clear, reading it aloud, discussing the passage with someone, etc.

> **Assessment point**
>
> Listen to individual children reading and make ongoing assessments on their decoding, sight vocabulary, approaches to tackling new words and their reading fluency. AF1

 After reading

Returning to the text

- What robot had Lucy designed and what special attributes did it have? **(recall)**
- How was Ant's Break-bot powered? **(recall)**
- Referring to the text, why didn't Ant's Break-bot win? **(recall, deducing, inferring and drawing conclusions)**
- Why do they think the competition organizers decided to award Ant a prize after all? **(synthesizing)**

> **Assessment point**
>
> Can the children describe why different things happened in the story, referring to the text? AF2/3

Building fluency

- Ask the children to take on one of the main characters. Go through the story together and ask them to rehearse the dialogue for their character, trying to ensure they use appropriate expression and intonation to bring out the meaning of the words.

> **Assessment point**
>
> Can the children read dialogue with expression and confidence, bringing out its meaning? AF1

Building comprehension

- Ask the children to draw a large circle, divide it into six sections – the number of chapters in the book – then write each chapter heading above one of the sections. The children then complete the summary wheel for the story by noting down the key events in the sections under the chapter headings. **(summarizing)**

- Using their notes, ask the children, in pairs, to take a chapter in turn and retell the story to each other. Encourage them to use story language as much as possible. **(recall, summarizing, determining importance, visualizing)**

> **Assessment point**
> Can the children retell the story, using story language? **AF2**

Chapter 4 – Strictly come robot-ing

The cinema was packed with children and robots. At the front, there was a model of Robo-Rex. Three judges were also on the stage, sitting behind a big desk. They were looking down at everyone.

"They make me nervous," said micro-size Tiger.

Tiger was hidden in the leg of the robot. Cat was working the arms. Max was in the head.

"Don't worry," whispered Ant. "When we're dancing, just do what I do."

Ant looked around the room. He spotted Lucy, a girl from school. She was a show-off. A crowd of people were standing around her. She was holding a sleek, shiny, pink robot.

"What's so special about her robot?" Cat wondered.

"Nothing to worry about," Ant whispered to his friends inside Break-bot.

"Are you sure?" Max said, peering through Break-bot's eyes.

Ⓦ Look at the email on page 31. Using *Ant's email* Photocopy Master, ask the children to write an email to the judges. Discuss some possible responses Ant might give. Remind them why it is important to fill in the 'To' and 'Subject' fields.

Assessment point

Can the children write an email, responding in an appropriate way? AF2

From:	The Judges
To:	Ant
Subject:	Amazing Robot Competition

Dear Ant,

We're really sorry we couldn't make you the winner yesterday. However, we think that Break-bot was really amazing, so we are sending you free passes to see the film studio where *Robo-Rex Comes Alive!* was made. You'll also meet Steve Spangler and Katie Winsome, of course!

Best wishes,
The Judges
Amazing Robot Competition

Follow-up activities

Writing activities
- Ask the children to look at their favourite section in the story and change some of the dialogue of the characters to thought bubbles. How does the text and punctuation need to change? **(short writing task)**
- Write an email inviting people to enter a competition to design a robot. The children will need to explain what sort of robots they are looking for, what the prize will be, and so on. **(longer writing task)**
- Ask the children to design and draw a robot. Ask them to label its features and write a short description about what makes their robot special. **(short writing task)**

Other literacy activities
- Create your own class competition for designing a robot. Give each member of the group or class roles to carry out. Promote the competition with posters and adverts, appoint judges, give feedback to entrants and work as a team. **(speaking and listening)**

Cross-curricular and thematic opportunities
- Work as a group to plan, design and build a giant robot. **(DT)**
- In small groups, the children could research one break-dancing move on the Internet and attempt to practise and perform it to the class. **(PE)**
- Explore manufactured robots that use control technology. **(ICT)**

Flying Machines

BY JOHN MALAM

About this book
This non-fiction book looks at the history of flight from Leonardo da Vinci's ideas of flying machines to modern planes that fly into space.

Writing genres:
non-chronological reports, charts, lists

You will need
- *Flying phonemes* Photocopy Master 20, *Teacher's Resource Book Age 6–9*
- *Help wanted!* Photocopy Master 21, *Teacher's Resource Book Age 6–9*

	Literacy Framework objective	Target and assessment focus
Speaking, listening, group interaction and drama	○ Listen to others in class, ask relevant questions and follow instructions **2.1**	○ We can listen to each other and ask relevant questions **AF2**
Reading	○ Read whole books on their own, choosing and justifying selections **8.1** ○ Explain their reactions to texts, commenting on important aspects **8.3**	○ We can describe why we chose different sections of the book **AF6** ○ We can comment on how useful the features of an information book are **AF4**
Writing	○ Draw on knowledge and experience of texts in deciding and planning what and how to write **9.1**	○ We can produce information pages that have important features of information texts such as charts, captions and bullet points **AF2**

Before reading

To activate prior knowledge
- What different flying machines do the children know about? Give them a large piece of paper to share and ask them to begin a concept map that shows what they already know about flying machines. **(activating prior knowledge)**
- What type of book is *Flying Machines*?

To preview the text and encourage prediction
- Look at the section headings on the contents page. Can the children use the headings to discuss what information about flying machines they might find in the book? **(previewing, predicting)**

To support decoding and word recognition and introduce new vocabulary
- **Phonic opportunity** Give the children the *Flying phonemes* Photocopy Master. Ask them to cut out the cards with the unusual names on them and use their phoneme knowledge to try to read them. The children can then check the pronunciation of the names in the book.
- You may also wish to point out some of the high or medium frequency words or practise decoding some of the phonically regular words in this book listed in the vocabulary chart on page 11.
- Before children read independently, ask them to rehearse what they might do if they become stuck on a word or sentence. The range of possible strategies (such as rereading, reading on, using context, using phonic, syntactic and vocabulary knowledge) should be well established for most readers and only an occasional reminder should be necessary.

During reading

- Ask the children to choose two sections from the contents page that most interest them to read.
- When they have finished reading these sections, ask them to use the index to find information about different subjects quickly. For example, can they find information about Charles Kettering or the Stealth Bomber?
- Stress the importance of comprehension, reminding the children to stop and take action if they are failing to understand the text, e.g. checking the meaning of a particular word or phrase, rereading more carefully, reading on to see if the meaning becomes clear, reading it aloud, discussing the passage with someone, etc.

··>

Assessment point

Listen to individual children reading and make ongoing assessments on their decoding, sight vocabulary, approaches to tackling new words and their reading fluency. **AF1**

 After reading

Returning to the text

- Ask the children why they chose the particular sections they did. **(personal response)**
- Did they enjoy the sections? Why or why not? **(personal response, adopting a critical stance)**

··>

Assessment point

Can the children express preferences and explain why they chose particular sections? **AF6**

- What do they notice about the index? Is it in a particular order? **(recall)**
- What different information features did they find on their pages? How useful were they? **(synthesizing)**
- What new information have they found out about flying? **(summarizing)**

··>

Assessment point

Can the children comment on the usefulness of the information features? **AF4**

Building vocabulary

- Ask the children to look up some of the emboldened words in the glossary. Can they find any other words in the text they think could go in the glossary? e.g. *glider*, *mission*, *unmanned*. Together, you could create glossary definitions for these words.

Building fluency and comprehension

- Invite the children to reread one of their chosen sections aloud to help the rest of the group understand the information.
- Ask the children to revisit the concept maps they began at the beginning of the book. What new information can they add to the map? **(synthesizing)**
- Ask the children to work together to develop other questions that they would like to find out about flying machines. Encourage them to listen to each other's questions and then make a final list of questions that would be the most useful to research. **(questioning)**

Assessment point
Can the children listen carefully to each other's suggestions? **AF2**

Ask the children to use their knowledge gained from reading this book to create a section about flying machines. The section should include a range of non-fiction features such as charts, captions and bullet points.

> **Assessment point**
>
> Can the children produce an information text that includes non-fiction features? **AF2**

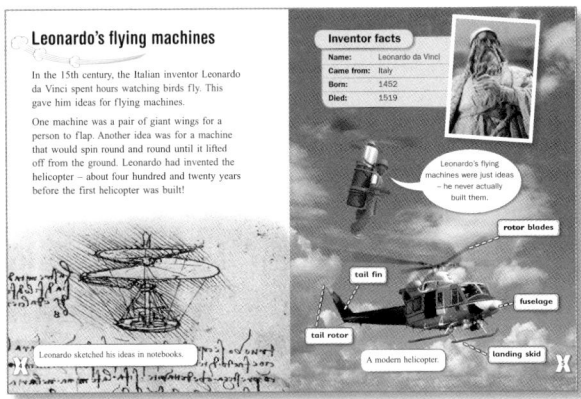

Follow-up activities

Writing activities

- Ask the children to complete the concept map about flying machines. **(short writing task)**
- Give out the *Help wanted* Photocopy Master to the children and ask them to list other words/information from the book that could be added to the index. They then need to write the page number where the information can be found. The children could swap their indexes with a partner to see if they were correct. **(short writing task)**
- Encourage the children to research the list of questions they created in books and on the Internet. They could then each write a section, adding the information they have discovered. Later on, the group could compile an index for their completed sections. **(longer writing task)**

Other literacy activities

- Delegate sections of the book to different pairs of children. Ask them to read the information in their section quietly together, then bring the group together and invite members to ask each other questions about the sections. **(speaking and listening)**

Cross-curricular and thematic opportunities

- Find out more about the history of flying. Ask the children to consider how each aircraft influenced life at the time. **(History)**
- Design a flying machine, ensuring that it has some features to enable it to fly, such as propellers. The children could invent an appropriate name for it. **(DT)**
- Design an image for a kite. **(Art and design)**
- Identify the countries which are mentioned in the book on a globe. **(Geography)**
- Encourage the children to research animals and insects that fly. Ask them to categorize them by sorting them into groups according to the shape of their wings. Look at unusual wings, such as dragonfly wings and bat wings. **(Science)**

Extreme Exploring Machines

BY ALISON BLANK

About this book
This book describes how new inventions have been developed to explore extreme environments.

Writing genres: non-chronological reports, labelled diagrams, captions

You will need
- *Explore or not to explore?* Photocopy Master 22, *Teacher's Resource Book Age 6–9* (enlarged)
- *Compare and contrast information* Photocopy Master 86, *Teaching Handbook Age 6–7* (Year 2/P3)
- Books/films/magazines/web links on environments mentioned in the book, e.g. volcanoes, planets (Mars), ocean floor, Antarctica (optional)

	Literacy Framework objective	Target and assessment focus
Speaking, listening, group interaction and drama	○ Listen to each other's views and preferences, agree the next steps to take and identify contributions by each group member **3.3**	○ We can work together as a group, listen to each other and make a team decision **AF3**
Reading	○ Engage with books through exploring and enacting interpretations **8.2**	○ We can explore and discuss the important issues in a book **AF7**
	○ Explain their reactions to texts, commenting on important aspects **8.3**	○ We can compare and contrast information from different sources **AF2/6**
Writing	○ Draw on knowledge and experience of texts in deciding and planning what and how to write **9.1**	○ We can write a persuasive letter **AF2**

Before reading

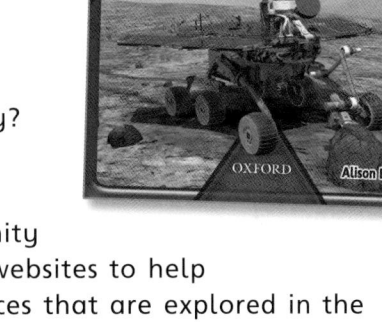

To activate prior knowledge and encourage prediction

- Look at the front cover. What do the children think the image might be of? **(predicting)**
- Look at the section headings on the contents page. Which extreme place would they most like to explore? Why? **(activating prior knowledge, personal response)**
- If possible, give children the opportunity to look at books, films, pictures and websites to help them to get to know some of the places that are explored in the book. Provide small world materials to allow them to explore their own worlds. **(building prior knowledge)**

To support decoding and word recognition and introduce new vocabulary

- You may wish to point out some of the high or medium frequency words or practise decoding some of the phonically regular words in this book and listed in the vocabulary chart on page 11.

To engage readers and model fluent reading

- Read pages 2 and 3 to the children. Demonstrate leaving pauses after reading a question to allow the listener to think about the questions being posed. What other questions would the children like to ask?
- Before children read independently, ask them to rehearse what they might do if they become stuck on a word or sentence. The range of possible strategies (such as rereading, reading on, using context, using phonic, syntactic and vocabulary knowledge) should be well established for most readers and only an occasional reminder should be necessary.

During reading

- Ask the children to choose three sections from the contents page that they would like to read. Explain that they will also need to read the final section on page 22.
- As they read, ask them to think of any questions they would like to ask an expert.
- Stress the importance of comprehension, reminding the children to stop and take action if they are failing to understand the text, e.g. checking the meaning of a particular word or phrase, rereading more carefully, reading on to see if the meaning becomes clear, reading it aloud, discussing the passage with someone, etc.

> **Assessment point**
>
> Listen to individual children reading and make ongoing assessments on their decoding, sight vocabulary, approaches to tackling new words and their reading fluency. AF1

 After reading

Returning to the text

- Ask the children what made them choose the sections they did. **(personal response, including adopting a critical stance)**
- Can the children remember what each extreme exploring machine was used for? **(recall, summarizing)**
- Where is Lake Vostok? Why do the children think the author has raised the issue of whether these types of lakes should be explored? **(deducing, inferring and drawing conclusions, personal response, including adopting a critical stance)**

Exploring in the future

Many people are excited about exploring the hidden lakes of Antarctica. Many others are worried about the damage that the exploration might do. They think that the lakes should be left alone and any life there should not be disturbed. What do you think?

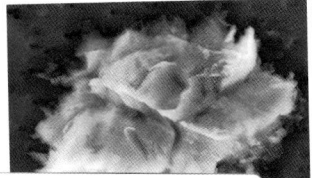

This picture shows magnified **micro-organisms** that were found in Lake Vostok – 3 kilometres (2 miles) below the ice sheet of Antarctica.

The challenge that scientists face is to explore new places without spoiling them. Future exploring machines will need to help us learn about our planet while protecting it for the future.

- Using an enlarged copy of the *Explore or not to explore?* Photocopy Master ask the children to contribute arguments towards whether or not scientists should explore extreme environments. Write the arguments under the headings and ask the children, as a group, to decide on the best wording to use. **(synthesizing, personal response, including adopting a critical stance)**

⋯⋯⋯⋯⋯⋯⋯⋯⋯⋯⋯⋯⋯▶

> **Assessment point**
>
> Can the children discuss and debate important issues raised by the author? **AF7**
>
> Can they work together as a team to decide how their arguments should be written? **AF3**

- Depending on each child's viewpoint, ask them to write a short letter to NASA to persuade them to design a new machine to explore a different planet, or stop exploring new places to avoid damaging the earth. Remind them to use or adapt the arguments that you listed as a group.

⋯⋯⋯⋯⋯⋯⋯⋯⋯⋯⋯⋯⋯▶

> **Assessment point**
>
> Can the children write a persuasive letter, listing their arguments which reflect their viewpoint? **AF2**

Building comprehension

- Ask the children to think of questions they would like to ask an expert to find out more about the unusual environments they have explored. **(questioning)**
- Allow them to choose the environment they are most interested in and provide them with books, magazines and websites to explore the environment in greater depth. Ask the children to complete a *Compare and contrast information* Photocopy Master, listing the different sources they have used. **(synthesizing)**
- What new environments do they think might be left to discover? **(predicting)**

⋯⋯⋯⋯⋯⋯⋯⋯⋯⋯⋯⋯⋯▶

> **Assessment point**
>
> Can the children compare and contrast different sources of information? **AF2/6**

Follow-up activities

Writing activities
- Write a short description of an imaginary super machine that has been designed to explore a new extreme environment. Give the machine an appropriate name. **(short writing task)**
- Create a labelled diagram of the super machine, giving technical information about the machine. They could use the captions for the diagram on pages 6 and 7 as a model for the style of writing. **(short writing task)**
- Ask the children to use their notes on the *Compare and contrast information* Photocopy Master to compile an information text about their chosen extreme environment. These could be displayed in the classroom for other children to read. **(longer writing task)**

Other literacy activities
- Work as a group to create a TV broadcast describing the day your new super machine is used to explore an extreme environment. Ensure each member of the group has a role and works as part of a team. **(speaking and listening)**

Cross-curricular and thematic opportunities
- Design a machine to explore a different environment, e.g. a mountain terrain, underground cave, or a planet other than Mars. **(DT)**
- Explore the different planets in the solar system. Which ones would the children like to visit? Why? Can the children find out what particular conditions the planets have that make exploration difficult? **(Science)**
- Look at different explorers through history. What different lands did they discover? What different machines and inventions did they use to help them? **(History, Science, Geography)**